This memory journal
belongs to:

_____

_____

_____

I was so blessed to have you in my life

A Father's
Love is
Forever

In Loving Memory Of

_____

_____

_____

Born

_____

Departed

_____

A brief summary of who my Dad was

About My Dad

_____

_____

_____

_____

_____

_____

_____

About My Dad

_____

_____

_____

_____

_____

_____

_____

About My Dad

_____

_____

_____

_____

_____

_____

_____

About My Dad

_____

_____

_____

_____

_____

_____

_____

About My Dad

_____

_____

_____

_____

_____

_____

_____

_____

About My Dad

_____

_____

_____

_____

_____

_____

_____

My Memories

My Memories

My Memories

My Memories

My Memories

 # My Memories

_____

_____

_____

_____

_____

_____

_____

_____

_____

_____

_____

_____

_____

_____

_____

_____

_____

_____

My Memories

My Memories

My Memories

My Memories

My Memories

My Memories

My Memories

 # My Memories

_____

_____

_____

_____

_____

_____

_____

_____

_____

_____

_____

_____

_____

_____

_____

_____

_____

_____

_____

_____

My Memories

My Memories

My Memories

My Memories

My Memories

 # My Memories

_____

_____

_____

_____

_____

_____

_____

_____

_____

_____

_____

_____

_____

_____

_____

_____

_____

My Memories

My Memories

My Memories

My Memories

My Memories

My Memories

My Memories

My Memories

My Memories

My Memories

My Memories

My Memories

♥♥ My Memories ♥♥

 # My Memories

_____

_____

_____

_____

_____

_____

_____

_____

_____

_____

_____

_____

_____

_____

_____

_____

_____

_____

My Memories

My Memories

❤ My Memories ❤

My Memories

My Memories

My Memories

My Memories

My Memories

My Memories

My Memories

My Memories

My Memories

My Memories

 # My Memories

_____

_____

_____

_____

_____

_____

_____

_____

_____

_____

_____

_____

_____

_____

_____

_____

My Memories

My Memories

My Memories

My Memories

My Memories

My Memories

My Memories

My Memories

My Memories

My Memories

My Memories

My Memories

My Memories

 My Memories

My Memories

My Memories

My Memories

My Memories

My Memories

My Memories

My Memories

My Memories

My Memories

My Memories

My Memories

My Memories

My Memories

My Memories

My Memories

My Memories

My Memories

My Memories

My Memories

My Memories

My Memories

My Memories

Letters to Heaven

# Letters to Heaven

Letters to Heaven

Letters to Heaven

Letters to Heaven

Letters to Heaven

Letters to Heaven

Letters to Heaven

Letters to Heaven

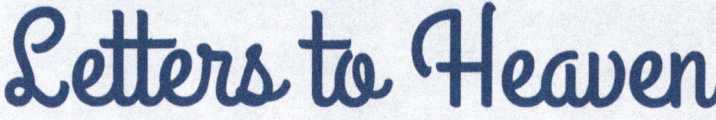

Letters to Heaven

Thank-you for loving me and for all the great times

I will treasure the photos, lessons, family memories, and all that we shared and all that you taught me.

I love you Dad
& will remember
you always

Rest easy...

Until we meet
again!

Made in the USA
Coppell, TX
07 August 2023

20051186R00063